Published by Evans Brothers Limited
2A Portman Mansions
Chiltern Street
London W1U 6NR

First published 2004

Printed in China

British Library Cataloguing in Publication data.

Powell, Jillian
Becky has diabetes. - (Like Me, Like You)
1. Diabetes - Juvenile literature 2. Diabetics - Juvenile
literature
I. Title
618.9'2462

ISBN 0237526611

Acknowledgements

The author and publisher would like to thank the following
for their help with this book:

Becky, Natalie, Linda and Jason McGovern and Francesca
Smith.

Thanks also to the Juvenile Diabetes Research Foundation
for their help in preparation of this book.

All photographs by Gareth Boden

Credits

Series Editor: Louise John
Editor: Julia Bird
Designer: Mark Holt
Production: Jenny Mulvanny

Juvenile
Diabetes
Research
Foundation

dedicated to finding a cure

Becky has
DIABETES

JILLIAN POWELL

Evans

Hi, my name is Becky and I have diabetes. It means my body doesn't make **insulin** so I run out of energy sometimes. I have to have two **injections** of insulin a day, but I'm used to them now.

6

DIABETES

There are two types of diabetes. Children usually have type 1 diabetes, which means they need injections of insulin.

I live with my mum, my dad, my sister Natalie and all our pets. We've got two cats, a hamster and two fish! I love animals, and I also like riding my scooter, drawing and playing on the computer.

I share a bedroom with Natalie. Mum wakes us up in the morning. I have to wash my hands, then do my blood test. It's quite easy. I prick my finger and squeeze a drop of blood on to the test paper.

The test tells me my **blood sugar level.** If my blood sugar level is low, I eat a bigger breakfast. I have to do a blood test before every meal. I write down the results in this book.

9

Now it's time for my insulin injection. Dad usually does my injections but I'm learning to do them myself. This morning I'm having the injection in my arm. Dad gives me the injection before he goes to work. I need to have it before I eat my breakfast.

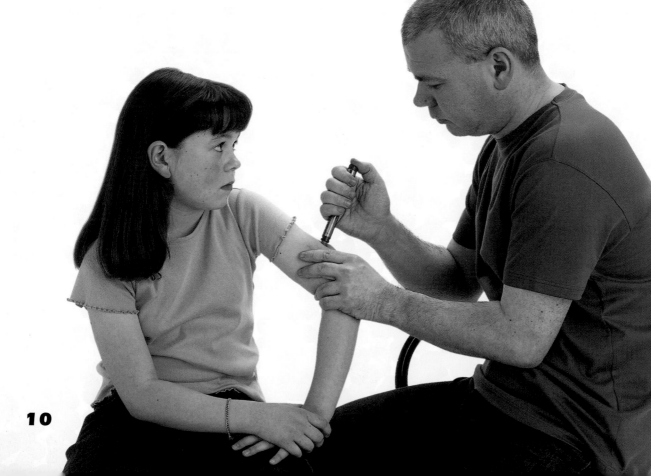

10

My blood sugar level was okay this morning so I'm just having a bowl of cereal for breakfast. Because I have diabetes, I can't normally eat foods that have a lot of sugar in them. Mum always checks to see how much sugar there is in my food.

INSULIN

Insulin is normally made in our bodies. It helps our bodies use sugar from food to give us energy. When someone has diabetes, their body doesn't make enough insulin, so too much sugar stays in their blood.

Today I'm going to the park with my friend Francesca. I have to remember to pack everything I need. I always carry my **blood test kit** and some chocolate and glucose tablets in case my blood sugar level gets too low.

12

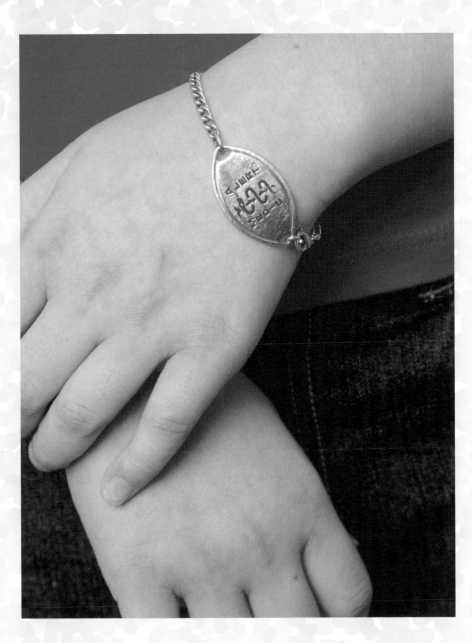

I always wear this special bracelet, too. It tells people that I have diabetes. If my blood sugar level got very low and I was ill, someone could ring the number on my bracelet to get help quickly.

Francesca's here! We're going to take our scooters to the park. We'll be using up lots of energy, so I must make sure I eat my packed lunch. I'll also have some snacks so my blood sugar level doesn't get too low.

14

Francesca always checks to see if I'm feeling okay. She's brought some chocolate bars in case I need one. But she tries not to eat too many sweets in front of me because she knows I can't have them as often as she can!

Mum has packed me a healthy lunch. I've got cheese and biscuits and a low-fat yoghurt. I can eat most things, except for foods that have a lot of sugar or fat like cakes, biscuits and fizzy drinks.

Today we're going to have an ice cream for a treat. I can't eat ice cream very often because it has quite a lot of sugar in it. Sometimes I have a sugar-free lolly instead.

On the way home, we stop at a shop to buy some sweets. I keep some in a box at school in case my blood sugar level gets low. Francesca helps me choose some.

Francesca has to go home soon but she comes back to my house to see my new fish first. He's called Fizzle!

Later, when Francesca has gone, I tell Dad I'm feeling a bit **'hypo'**. This happens when my blood sugar level is getting low. Sometimes it happens when I've been using lots of energy, but it can happen anytime – even when I'm in bed at night.

20

FEELING 'HYPO'

When someone with diabetes feels hypo, they may look pale and feel tired, dizzy and shaky.

I feel dizzy and my hands get a bit shaky. Dad tells me to do a blood test to see how low my blood sugar level is. He gives me some juice to bring the level back up. Then Mum makes me a snack.

Mum rings my teacher to remind her I have a check-up at the hospital in the morning, so I'll be a bit late to school. I usually have a check-up four times a year.

I don't mind going to the check-ups now. I know the doctor and the nurse. They weigh and measure me and look through my blood sugar results. We also talk about the best foods for me to eat.

Before I go to bed, I do another blood test. Then Mum makes me some toast so my blood sugar level doesn't get too low when I'm asleep.

I can sometimes wake up feeling a bit hypo, so I keep a basket by my bed with everything I need inside.

When I first got diabetes, I was very ill and I had to go into hospital to have lots of tests. I felt a bit scared, but I don't mind too much now. I've got used to the injections and making sure I eat when I need to.

Having diabetes doesn't stop me from doing all my favourite things – like having water fights with Francesca!

Glossary

Blood sugar level the amount of sugar carried in someone's blood

Blood test kit a kit for testing the amount of sugar in the blood

Hypo (hypoglycaemic) how someone feels when their blood sugar level is too low

Injection having a needle prick to put something into the blood

Insulin a chemical made in the body that controls the amount of sugar in the blood

Index

Further Information

Juvenile Diabetes Research Foundation
Tel: 020 7713 2030
www.jdrf.org.uk
JDRF is dedicated to finding a cure for type 1 diabetes, and its complications through the support of research. Until a cure is found, JDRF seeks to provide information on research developments and different aspects of living with diabetes through publications, information leaflets and educational events.

UNITED KINGDOM
Diabetes UK
Tel: 020 7424 1000
www.diabetes.org.uk
Lots of information for children and adults with diabetes. Leaflets, videos, magazines and books on diabetes are also available.

UNITED STATES OF AMERICA
American Diabetes Association
Tel: 1 800 342 2383
www.diabetes.org
Information and support for people with diabetes.

AUSTRALIA
Diabetes Australia
Tel: 1300 136 588
www. diabetesaustralia.com.au
Practical advice and support for people with diabetes. Factsheets and magazines are available.

NEW ZEALAND
Diabetes New Zealand
Tel: 0800 342 238
www.diabetes.org.nz
Advice and tips on living with diabetes.

BOOKS
Body Systems: Eating and Digestion
Anita Ganeri, Heinemann Library 1997

Living with diabetes Jenny Bryan, Wayland Publishers 1998

What does it mean to have diabetes?
Louise Spilsbury, Heinemann Library 2002

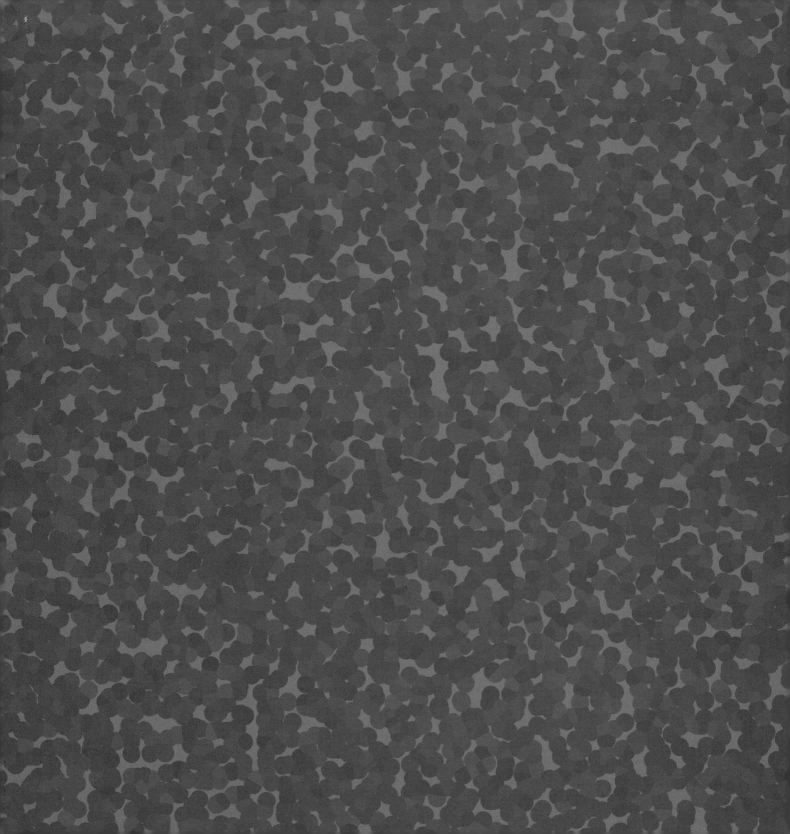